FOCUS ON THE FAMILY®

20 BIBLE VERSES

Every Child Should Know

with **20 original Bible memory songs on full-length CD**

illustrated by Christine Tripp
songs by Little Man Music

Standard
PUBLISHING
CINCINNATI, OHIO

Heritage Builders®

All songs © 2003 Little Man Music, Wheaton, Illinois (ASCAP).

Acknowledgements
Contributing writers: Kerry Kloth (An Endless Friend, Share God's Love, Upside-Down Van, Museum Mania, Trouble in the Tubes); JoDee McConnaughhay (I Made It Myself, The Do-Right Day, You're First With Me, A Promise You Can Use, What's the Recipe?); Clare Mishica (All Day Long, Sailing Away, In a Minute, Lost in Left Field, Hedgehogs and Sunshine); Tammy Nischan (Crossing the River, New Boy in Town, No Rain in the Forecast, An American Missionary, Easier Than You Think). Illustrator: Christine Tripp.

CD recorded and mixed by Mark Blas at Up on the Roof Studios, Lombard, Illinois. Assistant engineer: Nate Dunn. Mastered by John Morton at Music Precedent, Springfield, Missouri.

Singers: Scott Liebenow, Cathy Liebenow, Beth Maas, Cassie Peletis, James Skallerup, Richard Liebenow, Jeff Steurer, Joy Curry, Scott Graffius.

Musicians: Scott Liebenow (piano, keyboards, drums, percussion); Errol Brown (bass); Scott Graffius (guitar); Mike Priami (guitar); Andrew Wilson (percussion).

Soloists: Joy Curry (Love Your Neighbor, Love the Lord); Jeff Steurer (Listen to You); Scott Graffius (Yesterday, Today, Forever); Cassie Peletis (Worship the Lord); Beth Maas (Be Kind and Compassionate, Trust in the Lord); Jessica Kinsman (spoken prayer for Listen to You).

ISBN 0-7847-1411-8

09 08 07 06 05 04   9 8 7 6 5 4 3

20 Bible Verses Every Child Should Know

Table of Contents

Decide to Live for God

A NOTE TO PARENTS

Have you been looking for a fun, new resource to help your child learn Bible verses? Well, you've found it—and more! Your whole family will enjoy *20 Bible Verses Every Child Should Know.* It has fun-to-sing music, read-aloud stories, and simple-to-do activities that will inspire and challenge.

These 20 verses have been chosen to represent basic Bible concepts that should be a part of every child's life. They will strengthen your child's spiritual journey by encouraging him to discover who God is, desire a relationship with God, and decide to live for God.

For every Bible verse you will find:

— A brand-new memory song that contains a direct quote of the verse, including the reference, on a full-length stereo CD. Everyone in your family will enjoy the wonderful variety of music that has been especially written and recorded just for this project!

— A contemporary story that relates the verse to everyday life. Read it together and allow it to spark conversations with your child about her own similar experiences. (Don't forget to share *your* own stories, too!)

— Two memory boosters that suggest simple activities for learning and understanding the verse. Use them to create teachable moments as you guide your child toward making God's Word a natural part of life.

— Full lyrics for the Bible memory song to help you sing along with the CD. They make it easy to join your child in the fun of learning the Bible with music.

In the Beginning

In the beginning God created the heavens and the earth. GENESIS 1:1

I MADE IT MYSELF

Sarah planted the tiny petunia seed weeks ago. Patiently she watered the seed and set the pot in the sun every day. Slowly the seed sprouted and sent a little green shoot up through the soil. Then a tiny bud appeared. Sarah knew a blossom would soon unfold. And sure enough, it did! Sarah and Mother carried the blooming plant outside.

"Isn't it beautiful!" Mother exclaimed.

"Yes," said Sarah. She touched the velvet petals. "They're so soft and so purple!"

Mother smiled. "Sarah, who made our pretty petunia?"

"I did!" Sarah announced.

"You did?" Mother squeaked. That wasn't the answer she expected.

"Yes," said Sarah. "I watered it every day."

"Yes," said Mother, "but who made it grow?"

"I did," said Sarah.

"You did?" asked Mother.

"Yes," said Sarah. "I set it in the sun every day."

"But," said Mother, "who made it in the beginning?"

"I did," said Sarah.

"Oh, really?" asked Mother.

"Yes," said Sarah. "I planted the seed."

Mother thought a moment. "Then where did the seed come from?"

"Uhhhh," Sarah stammered. "The store, I guess?"

"Not in the beginning," said Mother. "Everything your petunia was going to be was already hidden in the seed before you planted it. Who is big enough and smart enough to make seeds like that in the first place?"

"God?" said Sarah in a wee voice.

"Yes, God!" Mother smiled. "And, who made the soil you planted the seed in?"

"God?" asked Sarah.

"Yes, God," said Mother. "And who made the water you poured on the seed to help it grow?"

"God," said Sarah.

"Yes, God," said Mother. "And who made the sun that gave your petunia the light it needed?"

"God again," said Sarah.

"Yes, God again," said Mother. "So, Sarah, who really made our pretty purple petunia?"

"God did!" Sarah laughed.

"Yes, God did!" Mother said. "But who was God's special helper?"

"Me?" Sarah giggled.

"Yes, you!" Mother said, hugging Sarah tight. "And I'm especially glad that God made you."

Now go back to the big picture and tell what Sarah learned about Genesis 1:1.

MEMORY BOOSTERS

★ Cover your eyes: "In the beginning" there was nothing. Look at the sky: "God created the heavens." Touch the earth: "God created the earth." Now say Genesis 1:1. Cover your eyes, point to the sky, and touch the earth at the right times.

★ Grow petunias or other flowers. Repeat Genesis 1:1 each time you care for them. Write Genesis 1:1 on a card, glue it to a stick, and poke it into the soil with the flowers.

IN THE BEGINNING

Chorus:
In the beginning (echo)
God created (echo)
The heavens (echo)
And the earth (echo)

(Repeat chorus)

He made the day and night
Twinkling stars and sun so bright
He made the land and seas
The pretty flowers and big, big trees

(Repeat chorus)

He made the birds that sing
The fish and every living thing
He made the first man
And God gave a wife to him

(Repeat chorus)

Where do all these things come from
It all starts with Genesis 1:1

(Repeat chorus)

Words and Music by Scott and Cathy Liebenow

The Lord Is My Shepherd

The Lord is my shepherd, I shall not be in want. PSALM 23:1

ALL DAY LONG

Syd and Aunt Kay hurried down to the beach with their picnic basket and blanket. Syd loved going on picnics with her aunt.

"Let's go and look for rocks," said Syd, excitedly pulling on Aunt Kay's arm.

"Sure," agreed Aunt Kay. The waves splashed in and Syd filled her pockets with pebbles. Then she spotted a glittery red one. She reached to grab it and tumbled right into the water.

"I'm all wet!" Syd shivered as Aunt Kay helped her up.

"Don't worry," said Aunt Kay. "I have an extra sweatshirt in the car."

Syd went to the car and quickly changed her wet shirt. "Your sweatshirt looks like a dress on me," she giggled.

Next, Syd and Aunt Kay went to eat their snack, but it was gone!

"Oh, no," said Aunt Kay. "The seagulls ate our sandwiches!"

Syd laughed and shoved her hands deep into the pockets of the sweatshirt. "Look what I found!" she exclaimed, holding up a pack of crackers.

"I forgot I had those," laughed Aunt Kay. "Let's eat."

As Aunt Kay and Syd finished their snack, the sky turned black. Raindrops plopped down—slowly at first, but then it began to pour.

"Hurry!" shouted Aunt Kay, taking Syd's hand and racing toward the car.

Thunder crashed and lightning flashed as they jumped into the car and pulled the doors closed behind them. Suddenly, a flash of lightning

 struck a nearby tree! It cracked and fell down across the car. The leafy branches blocked the car doors.

"Are you OK?" Aunt Kay asked Syd.

"I'm not hurt," said Syd in a shaky voice, "but I am afraid."

"When I'm afraid I say Psalm 23," said Aunt Kay. "It reminds me that God protects us. Will you help me say it out loud?"

Syd nodded and Aunt Kay started to pray. "The Lord is my shepherd, I shall not be in want."

Syd repeated the words, and she did feel better.

All at once, a fire truck pulled up. "Are you all right?" a fireman shouted.

"Yes, but the doors are jammed," answered Aunt Kay.

"We'll get you out," said the fireman. "A lady living on the hill saw your car and called us."

"Thank you," said Aunt Kay. By now, Syd's grip on Aunt Kay's hand was beginning to loosen.

"God did protect us," said Syd, "all day long!"

Now go back to the big picture and tell what Syd learned about Psalm 23:1.

MEMORY BOOSTERS

★ Say, "Let it rain!" and make "rain" by clapping your hands on your thighs. Shout, "Stop!" and say Psalm 23:1 together. Say, "Let it storm!" and create "thunder" by pounding your fists on your thighs. Shout, "Stop!" and say Psalm 23:1 together. Make up actions for other scary situations.

★ While talking with your child about the job of a shepherd, look at pictures of sheep. Then have him draw and cut out a sheep shape. Print the Bible verse on the shape. Hang the sheep where your child will be reminded of the verse often.

SHEPHERD SONG

When I am afraid
And there are lots of scary noises made
I know that God is with me
And He helps me to be strong

Chorus:
The Lord is my shepherd
I shall not be in want
Psalm twenty-three, verse one
The Lord is my shepherd
I shall not be in want
Psalm twenty-three, verse one

When you are afraid
And the sky is very dark and gray
Remember God is with you
And He'll help you to be strong

(Repeat chorus)

We don't need to fear
Jesus promised that He would be near
If Jesus lives inside our hearts
He's with us all the time

(Repeat chorus)

Psalm twenty-three, verse one

Words and Music by Scott Graffius

God Gave His Son

For God so loved the world that he gave his one and only Son, that whoever believes in him shall not perish but have eternal life. JOHN 3:16

THE DO-RIGHT DAY

Anna touched the rough wood of the homemade cross. It rested on the steps in the church worship area. "Watch for splinters," warned Daddy.

"Did Jesus get splinters?" asked Anna.

"I don't know," said Daddy. He picked up a thorny wreath to set on the cross.

"What's that?" asked Anna.

"It's a crown of thorns," said Daddy. "It's like the one Jesus wore the day He died."

"Did it hurt?"

"Yes," said Daddy.

"Daddy," said Anna, tears falling, "why did Jesus have to die?"

"Because we sin by doing what's wrong in God's sight," said Daddy. "We should be punished for our sin, but Jesus died so we would not be punished. Anyone who believes in and obeys Jesus won't be punished."

"If we didn't sin," said Anna, "would Jesus have to die?"

"Honey, we all sin. That's why we need Jesus."

Maybe if I do only right today, Anna thought, *then Jesus wouldn't have to die for me!*

At home, Anna kicked off her shoes and went to work doing right.

Anna's little sister took Anna's favorite stuffed puppy. Anna almost yanked it from her tiny hands.

Mom told Anna to put her socks in the drawer. Anna was playing and almost stuck them under her bed instead. At snack time, Daddy asked, "How much ice cream does Mom usually give you?" Anna almost said two scoops instead of one.

In a few hours, Anna almost hurt her sister, disobeyed her mother, and lied to her father. *Whew! I'm glad it's bedtime,* she thought. Daddy came to tuck her in. "Daddy," said Anna, "Jesus didn't have to die for me! I did right today."

"Oh," said Daddy. "I'm sure God is pleased that you're doing right, but Jesus still had to die."

"But I didn't do anything wrong!" Anna sniffled.

"Did you do something wrong yesterday?"

If it was like today, Anna thought, *I probably did.* "I guess . . ."

"Jesus died for the wrong we've done and for the wrong we'll do. He loves us that much. And remember, Jesus didn't stay dead. He came back to life and lives forever."

"Okay," Anna said. "But I did everything right today."

Bump! "Anna," Mom called, "you forgot to put your shoes away!"

"I'm sorry," Anna yelled. "Daddy, I guess I can't do everything right."

"Maybe not," said Daddy, "but Jesus will help when we ask."

So Anna prayed, "Thank You, Jesus, for dying for me. And please help me do right. I sure can't do it alone!"

Now go back to the big picture and tell what Anna learned about John 3:16.

MEMORY BOOSTERS

★ Draw a large heart shape on poster board. Write the words of John 3:16 in big letters inside the heart. Fill in the letters with bright colors. Cut the heart into puzzle-shaped pieces. Work the puzzle and say the verse!

★ Say John 3:16. Ask: Whom did God love? (The world!) Who is the world? (We are!) Repeat John 3:16. Ask: Whom did God give? (His only Son.) Who is His only son? (Jesus!) Repeat John 3:16. Ask: Who can have eternal life? (Whoever believes in Jesus!)

GOD SO LOVED THE WORLD

Chorus:
For God so loved the world that He gave
    His one and only Son
That whoever believes in Him shall not
    perish
But have eternal life

No matter what you've done
God will forgive
The battle's won
Jesus died upon the cross
So we'd be saved and not be lost

   (Repeat chorus)

So where do you think we'd find
This verse that's good for all mankind
It's easier than it may seem
Open your Bibles to John 3:16

   (Repeat chorus)

Words and Music by Scott Liebenow

23

Jesus Is the Way

Jesus answered, "I am the way and the truth and the life. No one comes to the Father except through me." JOHN 14:6

CROSSING THE RIVER

"Only three more hours until we leave for vacation!" Nick exclaimed as he tossed his shirts and shorts into his suitcase.

"Don't forget your swimming suit!" his mom reminded him from downstairs.

"That's right!" Nick replied excitedly. "We always go swimming when we go to Aunt Brenda's house." Spending time with his cousins, Ben and Thomas, was one of Nick's favorite things to do. He liked going with them to the beach where they spent hours building sandcastles and looking for shells.

Nick chuckled as he placed his suitcase beside his mom's. He was remembering a time when the trip used to frighten him instead of make him excited. "Mom," Nick said, "do you remember how scared I used to get when we went to Aunt Brenda's?"

"Yes," his mom responded with a smile. "One time you asked if we could take a plane so that we wouldn't have to drive over the bridge into Aunt Brenda's town."

Nick shook his head, a little embarrassed, and said, "Now that I am older, I know that the bridge is the only way into Aunt Brenda's town. And it is very safe."

Nick's family finished loading the car and everyone piled in. Then his dad prayed, "Dear God, please give us safety as we travel. And help us to please You in everything we do. We look forward to being with You in Heaven for eternity. In Jesus name, amen."

As they pulled out of the driveway and began down the road, Nick started to think about his dad's prayer. "Dad," said Nick, "I know that Heaven is a special place, but I'm not sure I understand how to get there."

Mom was listening to the conversation between Nick and his dad when she remembered the bridge that Nick had once feared. "Remember that bridge to Aunt Brenda's?" she chimed in. "It's the only way to get to her house, right?"

"Right," Nick replied.

"Well, Jesus is like that bridge," she continued. "He is our only way into Heaven. All He asks is that we love Him and obey Him. Then He will take us to Heaven just like the bridge takes us to Aunt Brenda's."

"Oh!" Nick exclaimed. "Jesus is like a bridge to Heaven. I wouldn't want to get there any other way!"

Now go back to the big picture and tell what Nick learned about John 14:6.

MEMORY BOOSTERS

★ Write a different phrase of John 14:6 on each of seven cards. For example, on the first card write "Jesus answered," and on the second card write "I am the way." Then mix up the cards and have your child place them in the correct order. He should say the complete verse when he is done.

★ Have your child say John 14:6 each time you cross a bridge together. If it's a long bridge, continue saying the verse until you reach the other side. If you have very few bridges to cross, use pictures and/or stories of bridges to prompt the recitation of this verse.

I AM THE WAY

There is only one way (one way)
To get to Heaven (one way)
It is through my friend (my friend)
His name is Jesus (Jesus)

When the people asked Him
How do ya get to Heaven
Jesus looked at them
And Jesus answered

Chorus:
I am the way and the truth and the life
No one comes to the Father except through me
I am the way and the truth and the life
No one comes to the Father except through me

Look in your Bibles (Bible)
At the book of John (chapter 14)
A very special verse (verse 6)
It answers the question (question)

What is the way
To get to the Father
That was the question
That Jesus answered

(Repeat chorus)

Words and Music by Scott and Cathy Liebenow

Jesus Is Always the Same

Jesus Christ is the same yesterday and today and forever.
HEBREWS 13:8

AN ENDLESS FRIEND

As kids poured out of school, Emily spotted her friend. "Ashley!" she called, running to where her friend sat on the school steps.

"Ashley, why didn't you sit with me at lunch?" Emily asked. "I saved you a seat."

"I was sitting with Nicole," replied Ashley. "I want to be friends with her now." Beep! Just then, Ashley's dad came and she ran away without another word.

Emily felt like crying. When her mom pulled up in their van, she crawled into the very back seat.

"Emily, how was school today?" her mom asked, smiling.

"OK," Emily muttered, sinking lower into her seat. Her mom was watching her in the rearview mirror.

At home Emily tried to eat her graham cracker snack. But she wasn't hungry. Her mom sat down with her. "Honey, what's wrong?"

Tears spilled down Emily's cheeks. "Ashley doesn't want to be my friend anymore. She said that she's friends with Nicole now."

Her mom held her as she cried. When Emily's tears slowed, her mom got up. "Stay here; I have something to show you."

As Emily sniffed back more tears, her mom brought over the big photo album. She pointed to a faded black and white picture. "Do you know who this is?" she asked.

"That's Grandma and Grandpa," said Emily. "They really look different."

"That's right," Mom said, turning pages. "And who is this cute, chubby baby?"

"Me," Emily smiled.

"Right again," said Mom. "Honey, everyone changes. Your grandparents used to be newlyweds and now they're retired in Florida. You were a baby who couldn't even speak, and now you're reading and playing soccer."

"But why do friends have to change?" Emily asked.

"I don't know, but sometimes people just change their minds," said Mom. "Then all you can do is find other friends and be the best friend you can be."

"But there *is* someone who never changes," Mom said with a smile. "Jesus! He loved you bunches when you were born, and He loves you today. He's a friend who will never leave you. The Bible says He is always the same."

"So I could ask Jesus to help me not be so sad about Ashley," Emily said quietly.

"Yes, ask Him," encouraged Emily's mom. "He's always there and ready to listen."

Now go back to the big picture and tell what Emily learned about Hebrews 13:8.

MEMORY BOOSTERS

⭐ In a family album, find an older and a newer photo of one person. Identify a way that person changed. Say, "_____ has changed by _____. Does Jesus ever change? No, Jesus is always the same." Then say Hebrews 13:8 together and choose more photos showing change.

⭐ Set a rhythmic pattern by clapping out a beat. Then say Hebrews 13:8 to the rhythm you've established. Allow your child to create a different rhythm each time she repeats the verse.

YESTERDAY, TODAY, FOREVER

Jesus Christ is the same
Yesterday and today and forever
Jesus Christ is the same
Yesterday and today and forever
(Now hop on your left foot . . . now the
right foot)
Hebrews 13:8
Hebrews 13, verse 8

Jesus Christ is the same
Yesterday and today and forever
Jesus Christ is the same
Yesterday and today and forever
(Clap your hands . . . and praise the Lord)
Hebrews 13:8
Hebrews 13, verse 8

Jesus Christ is the same
Yesterday and today and forever
Jesus Christ is the same
Yesterday and today and forever
(Jump up and down)
Hey! Hey! Hey! Hey!
Hebrews 13:8
Hebrews 13, verse 8

Music by Scott Graffius

God Loved Us First

We love because he first loved us. 1 JOHN 4:19

SHARE GOD'S LOVE

Legs pumping, houses flew by as Jaron pedaled his bike home. "Dad, Dad!" he called as he jumped off the bike and let it fall on the ground. He ran into the garage where his dad was working.

"Guess what?" Jaron said excitedly. "Someone bought Mrs. Schmidt's house and I think they have kids! Can I take them some cookies?"

Jaron's Sunday school teacher had asked them to find ways to share God's love and he thought this was a good way.

"Go ahead. I have to finish fixing this lawnmower," his dad said. "Then I'll come and meet them, too."

After his mom gave him some cookies, Jaron jumped on his bike and rode down the street. As he got closer to the house, he saw a boy about his own age. But something was different. This boy wasn't running or biking like Jaron. He was walking very slowly, holding a metal pole in each hand to help him.

Jaron stopped. He didn't know what to do. The boy wasn't like Jaron at all. *What can I say to a boy like that?* Jaron wondered.

Slowly, Jaron turned his bike around. On the way home he saw his dad walking. "So, did you meet our new neighbors?" Dad asked. "Do they have boys?"

"They have a boy, but he's, uh, different," he said. "He walks funny. I don't know what to say to him."

"Sometimes it's hard to get to know new people," Dad said. "Sometimes it's even scary. But that's a way we can share God's love. We can stretch ourselves to make friends with someone who's not like us."

Jaron and his dad walked back down the street. The boy and a girl were sitting on the front steps.

"Hi, I'm Jaron," he said shyly. "I live down the street. Here are some cookies for you."

"Hey, thanks!" the boy said. "My name's Matt and this is my sister, Kayla. I was hoping other boys lived on this street. Do you like to play chess?"

"I love chess," said Jaron. "I don't play much because my brother's too young."

"So is my sister," Matt said. "Do you want to play sometime?"

"Sure," said Jaron, grinning. Maybe this new boy wasn't so different after all. He was glad he chose to share God's love with this new friend.

Now go back to the big picture and tell what Jaron learned about 1 John 4:19.

MEMORY BOOSTERS

★ Help your child make a treat to share with someone in your neighborhood. As you work, talk with him about ways to show God's love. Ask questions that will help cue his response to be: "We love because he first loved us" 1 John 4:19.

★ While watching television together, make a game of finding people who are showing love to others. The first person to find someone shouts, "1 John 4:19!" and says the entire verse.

BECAUSE HE FIRST LOVED US

Are you big or are you small
Are you short or are you tall
Do you like to run and play
Or sit inside and dream all day
God is faithful, loving too
I want to be the same for you

Chorus:
God gives love from above
God loves you and I do too
Why
We love because He first loved us
1 John 4:19

Are you from far away
Or right here in the USA
It doesn't matter where you are
His love stretches very far
God's love for us will never end
And that's why I love you my friend

(Repeat chorus twice)

1 John 4:19
1 John 4:19
1 John 4:19

Words and Music by Scott and Cathy Liebenow

Love the Lord Your God

Love the Lord your God with all your heart and with all your soul and with all your strength. DEUTERONOMY 6:5

SAILING AWAY

Ben jumped into his cardboard box with his dinosaur and blanket. His dog, Pepper, jumped in, too.

"We're going to sail around the world," Ben told Pepper. Then he used his toy fishing pole and turned his blanket into a sail.

"Look at the dolphins," Ben giggled as he pointed to the pillows. "And there's a couch whale, too," he told Pepper.

Pepper hopped out and ran over to the shelf where Mom kept some nice things.

"Look out for the sea monster, Pepper!" called Ben. "I'll have to save you!"

Ben jumped out and scooped up Pepper. Then Ben spotted his mother's clown statue on the shelf.

"I'll save the clown, too," Ben giggled as he grabbed it.

Suddenly, Pepper wiggled and Ben's hand slipped. The clown flew out of his hand, breaking as it hit the floor.

"Oh, no!" Ben cried as he stared at the pieces. "Mom is going to be upset!"

"Come on," Ben told Pepper. "We're going to move away." Then he took the box onto the back porch and shut the door.

"This box is our cave," Ben said to Pepper. "We'll hide so that no one finds us." But Ben didn't feel happy about his new game.

"Ruff!" Pepper barked. He didn't like the cave game either.

All at once, someone pulled up the box.

"There you are," said Mom. "Do you know what happened to my statue?"

"I was hiding in my cave with Pepper," said Ben. "I don't know." Ben stared at his shoes. His stomach felt all mixed up like a box of puzzle pieces.

"It sounds like Pepper is tired of hiding," said Mom.

"Yes," said Ben. A tear slid down his cheek. "Hiding's not much fun . . . but I was afraid because I dropped your clown. I'm sorry."

"Thank you for telling me the truth," said Mom as she reached out and gave Ben a hug. "I love you, and when you tell the truth, you show God that you love Him."

Ben started to smile. "Loving God feels much better than hiding," he said, giving Mom his box. "You can use this for the pieces."

"OK," said Mom, smiling. "Then would you like to go to the park?"

"Yes!" cheered Ben. That question was easy to answer.

Now go back to the big picture and tell what Ben learned about Deuteronomy 6:5.

MEMORY BOOSTERS

★ Say Deuteronomy 6:5 together as you have breakfast. Talk with your child about ways to love God with all her heart in the coming day. Say the verse together again at dinner. Talk about ways you each loved God throughout the day.

★ Practice tapping out rhythms as you say Deuteronomy 6:5 together. Use your hands, feet, legs, and arms. To increase the difficulty, try emphasizing a different word each time you say the verse. You can also vary the speed of the tapping.

LOVE THE LORD

Chorus:
Love the Lord with all your heart
With all your soul
And with all your strength
Love the Lord with all your heart
With all your soul
And with all your strength

How can you show love to the Lord
You can pray and read your Bible every day
You can tell the truth
Be kind to your friends
You can sing out loud
Let your praise never end
Shout out His name
Let your voice come alive
With Deuteronomy 6:5

(Repeat chorus)

Love the Lord (8 times)

Words and Music by Scott Liebenow

Give Thanks to the Lord

Give thanks to the Lord, for he is good; his love endures forever.
PSALM 107:1

NEW BOY IN TOWN

Todd's first day of school in the new town wasn't at all like his dad had said it would be, with new friends and fun things to do. No, Todd's first day was much more like he had imagined—long, scary hallways and unfriendly faces.

"Hey, you!" one boy shouted. "What planet are you from?" Todd dropped his head as he walked into the classroom. Sitting at his desk he noticed a note that said, "Whoever sits here loves Abby." Everyone laughed as Todd threw the note in the trash and returned to his seat.

At dinner, he told his parents about his horrible day. Dad reminded Todd that change is always tough. "We have to thank God even in the tough times," he said.

At bedtime, Todd's dad prayed, "Dear God, thank You for being with Todd at school. Please help him to make a new friend soon." Todd felt better as he fell asleep.

In the next few days at school Todd forgot his lunch, lost his homework, got a bad grade on his first test, and was chosen by the school bully as a target for all of his jokes.

Todd's dad continued to promise that things would get better and said, "Your mom and I have hard times, too, but when we feel discouraged, we trust God and thank Him for helping us."

Finally, the weekend arrived and Todd was happy just to have survived his first week of school. On Sunday, he and his family visited

a new church. When Todd walked into his Sunday school class, he was happy to see a boy from his class at school.

"Hi, my name is Caleb," the boy told Todd. "I saw you at school but was afraid to say 'Hi.'"

Todd grinned, "I'm the one who has been afraid." They began to talk and were amazed at how much they had in common. Todd loved to play baseball and soccer. So did Caleb!

On Monday, school didn't seem so scary. Todd had a friend! At lunch they shared their extra cookies. At recess Todd and Caleb played together. And after school, Todd went to Caleb's house to play.

At bedtime, Todd told his dad how much he liked Caleb and it was OK that they had moved. Then Todd prayed, "Dear God, thank You for my new friend, Caleb. And thank You for never changing and for always loving me."

That night Todd fell asleep with a smile on his face.

Now go back to the big picture and tell what Todd learned about Psalm 107:1.

MEMORY BOOSTERS

★ Make Psalm 107:1 into a chant. Adult: "Give thanks, give thanks, give thanks to who?" Child: "Give thanks to the Lord!" Adult: "For He, for He, for He is what?" Child: "For He is good!" Adult: "His love, His love, His love endures how long?" Child: "His love endures forever!"

★ Each time you encounter something that "ends" (vacation, a flower, favorite cereal, etc.), thank God for the experience and recite Psalm 107:1. Help your child get a glimpse of what it means that God's love endures forever.

GIVE THANKS TO THE LORD

Give thanks to the Lord
For He is good
His love endures forever

Give thanks to the Lord
For He is good
His love endures forever
Psalm 107:1

Hallelujah (4 times)

Give thanks to the Lord
For He is good
His love endures forever

Give thanks to the Lord
For He is good
His love endures forever
Psalm 107:1

Hallelujah (8 times)

Words and Music by Scott Liebenow

Trust in the Lord

Trust in the Lord with all your heart and lean not on your own understanding. PROVERBS 3:5

NO RAIN IN THE FORECAST

Erich loved his grandpa. His favorite memories were of riding alongside his grandpa on the tractor while they plowed the fields. The smell of fresh dirt and wild flowers filled the air as the plow blades broke through the ground, preparing it for the next crop.

After a hard day of farming, Grandpa and Erich liked to enjoy cold sodas on their way home. The long ride also gave them time to talk and laugh about many things. Grandpa always reminded Erich of God's beautiful creation. Grandpa was thankful to be a farmer.

One fall, as harvest time approached, Grandpa began to worry because the weather was very dry. The forecast promised no rain. Every day Erich and Grandpa drove by the wheat and noticed how dry it looked. Grandpa became more and more discouraged. He even stopped laughing and talking with Erich.

Instead, the two spent their time watching for rain and worrying about the drought. Grandpa didn't mention God and His creation anymore.

Erich became sad and worried, too. How would Grandpa pay his bills? Would they ever have fun on the farm again? How could he help his grandpa?

Erich decided to talk to his mom. "Grandpa is very worried about his wheat, Mom, and I am worried, too. What can I do to help Grandpa?"

His mom, who trusted God with all of her heart, looked at Erich and said, "Praying is sometimes all we can do to help the people we love.

You can't make it rain and you can't make the wheat grow, but you can ask God to help Grandpa not to worry."

Erich knew his mom was right. He began praying every day. "Dear God, I don't understand why it doesn't rain, but please help Grandpa not to worry about it. Help him to trust You."

One day the sky became very dark and raindrops began to fall. The wheat soaked up the rain and began to grow! As Grandpa and Erich looked at the wheat, Grandpa realized he should have trusted God. He said, "Our worry caused us to miss many fun days together."

Erich smiled and said, "I have been praying that we would not worry anymore, Grandpa. God heard my prayers and answered them in a really big way!"

Grandpa smiled, too. "Thank you, Erich," he said. "Your faith has reminded me to trust God and to stop worrying."

Now go back to the big picture and tell what Erich learned about Proverbs 3:5.

MEMORY BOOSTERS

★ Cut a heart from red paper and a cross from brown paper. Write the words of Proverbs 3:5 on the heart. Glue a craft stick on the cross and stand it up in some clay. Lean the heart on the cross to give a visual reminder of the verse and that trust is leaning on Jesus.

★ The next time you give your child a sandwich, ask what the bread is made from. Help her recall Erich's story about wheat. What did caring for the wheat help Erich and Grandpa learn to do? Say Proverbs 3:5 as a reminder to trust God.

TRUST IN THE LORD

We will trust in God our king
Ruler and maker of everything
Because He always will provide
Just remember Proverbs 3, verse 5

Chorus:
Trust in the Lord with all your heart
And lean not on your own understanding
Trust in the Lord with all your heart
Proverbs 3, verse 5

Confia en el Senor (trust in the Lord)
De todo corazon (with all your heart)
Confia en el Senor (trust in the Lord)
De todo corazon (with all your heart)

(Repeat chorus)

Tag:
Confia en el Senor
de todo corazon
Confia en el Senor
Confia

(Repeat tag and chorus)

Words and Music by Scott Liebenow

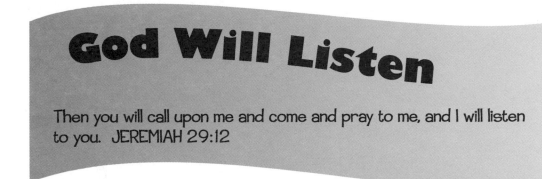

God Will Listen

Then you will call upon me and come and pray to me, and I will listen to you. JEREMIAH 29:12

UPSIDE-DOWN VAN

One morning on the way to school, Luke was watching a dump truck and a backhoe out his van window. Suddenly, he heard a loud, awful noise! The whole world seemed to be turning upside down! His van spun around and around and around until there was a huge crunch! Finally, the van stopped moving.

Luke found himself hanging sideways from the top of the van. Or at least it looked like the top. He began screaming and crying! His mom turned around and said as calmly as she could, "It's OK, Luke; it's OK."

The next few minutes were a blur as people came to help Luke and his mom out of the van. Sitting on the curb in his mom's arms, Luke watched police and fire trucks arrive. He even saw a helicopter circling overhead. He saw the crumpled front of the car that had hit them. He watched the tow truck lift their van from the middle of the road where it lay on its side.

After they visited the hospital and checked out OK, Luke's dad took him and Mom home. Luke didn't go to school that day. As he ate lunch and watched his favorite video, Luke almost forgot about the accident.

But as he slept that night, Luke had a bad dream. He saw a huge truck come out of nowhere and boom—hit his van! Luke sat straight up in bed crying, "Daddy, Daddy!"

"What's wrong, Buddy?" asked Luke's dad as he stumbled into the room.

"I had a scary dream about the accident," Luke said. "I never want to ride in a van again!"

Dad sat down on the edge of Luke's bed. "Son, it was an accident. Accidents don't happen very often. Your mom and I will do our best to keep from having another one."

"But, Daddy, that car hit us! What if another car hits us tomorrow?" Luke asked.

"It's true, son, we could have another accident. Some things in life are out of our control," said Dad. "But the Bible says if we pray to God, He'll listen to us. Let's ask God now to help you not be so scared and to keep us safe tomorrow."

"OK, Daddy. I know God will help me feel better," Luke said.

They bowed their heads together. And in his mind, Luke saw God leaning down to listen.

Now go back to the big picture and tell what Luke learned about Jeremiah 29:12.

MEMORY BOOSTERS

★ Use chenille wires to twist a body shape into being. Bend it so that it can rest on its knees. Mold the arms into a praying position. Hide the figure somewhere in the room. Each time your child finds it, repeat the words of Jeremiah 29:12 together.

★ Help your child make a list of things about which he can pray to God. Have him decorate the list and hang it near where he will see it at bedtime. Every night, recite Jeremiah 29:12 together and pray with your child about the things on his list.

LISTEN TO YOU

You can talk to me anywhere
I am here and you know I care
I will hear your prayers

I'm the maker of all things new
And no matter what you may do
I will still love you

So when you're sad just look to me
Open your heart get on your knees

Chorus:
Then you will call upon me
And come and pray to me
And I will listen to you listen to you
Then you will call upon me
And come and pray to me
And I will listen to you listen to you
This is Jeremiah 29:12

When you talk to me I hear you
Where you go I will be with you
I see everything you do

I made the wind and I made the rain
And I can help you through all your pain
My love will never change

So when you're sad just look to me
Open your heart get on your knees

(Repeat chorus)

Words and Music by Scott Liebenow

Worship the Lord

Worship the Lord your God and serve him only. LUKE 4:8

YOU'RE FIRST WITH ME

Slurp!

"Rusty!" Nathan said, waking to a wet puppy tongue.

"Time to get ready for church," said Mom from his doorway.

"Do we have to go?"

"You love your Sunday school class," said Mom. "Why would you want to miss it?"

"I don't want to leave Rusty alone," said Nathan.

"Rusty will be fine," said Mom. "You need to get ready now."

Later at lunchtime, it was Nathan's turn to pray.

"Dear God, thank You for the food. Amen," he said.

"Why the fast-food prayer, Nath?" asked Dad.

"I want to hurry so I can play with Rusty."

Then at Bible-reading time, Nathan begged, "Can we read just one verse and not the whole chapter?"

"What's the big hurry?" Dad asked.

"It's almost bedtime," said Nathan. "There's not much time left to play with Rusty."

The next weekend Nathan's little cousin, Hannah, visited. She giggled when Rusty licked her hand. Rusty followed her every move.

Nathan pouted while Rusty chased Hannah around the living room.

"Is it hard to share Rusty?" Mom asked.

"I want to share," said Nathan, "but Rusty is playing with Hannah and not me."

"How does that make you feel?" Mom asked.

"Sad—and kind of angry, too," said Nathan.

"I think God feels the same way," said Mom.

"Why?" Nathan asked.

"When you spend all your time thinking about someone or something else—even something as wonderful as a puppy—God notices. God wants us to give that kind of attention only to Him. That's called 'worship.'"

"Really?" asked Nathan.

"Yes," said Mom. "We worship God when we pray to Him. We worship God when we read His Bible. And we worship God when we praise Him together with our church family. If we quit doing those things, we show God that He is not important to us."

Mom left and Nathan prayed. "Dear God, I'm sorry I haven't paid attention to You lately. From now on, You're first with me. And—thank You for Rusty. He's a good dog, even if he forgot me."

Rusty dashed in and put his hot head on Nathan's knee.

Nathan smiled. "Most of all, God, thanks for wanting to spend time with me."

Now go back to the big picture and tell what Nathan learned about Luke 4:8.

MEMORY BOOSTERS

★ Have your child draw pictures of her favorite things. Now fold up the paper and write the words "God first" at the top. Say Luke 4:8 together. Help her thank God for all her favorite things and promise to keep "God first" in her life.

★ Write the words of the verse in alphabetical order. "They don't make sense that way, do they?" Say Luke 4:8. Talk about "priorities." Discuss with your child how she can show God that He is her "first" priority.

WORSHIP THE LORD

Clap your hands (clap, clap, clap)
Sing a song (la, la, la)
Bang on the drum (boom, boom, boom)
And hum along (hmm, hmm, hmm)
We're worshiping the Lord

Chorus:
Worship the Lord your God
And serve Him only
Luke chapter four, verse eight

Grizzly bears (roar)
And kangaroos (boing, boing)
Praise the Lord (praise the Lord)
And we can too (we can too)
We're worshiping the Lord

(Repeat chorus)

The best way to worship God
Is by living every day
Trying to do our best
To please Him in every way

Skip down the hall
Dance on the floor
So many ways
To praise the Lord
We're worshiping the Lord

(Repeat chorus)

Words and Music by Scott Graffius

Jesus Gives Me Strength

I can do everything through him who gives me strength.
PHILIPPIANS 4:13

A PROMISE YOU CAN USE

Riley gripped the rainbow picture he'd made for Great-grandma. He loved to draw rainbows. Rainbows reminded Riley that God keeps His promises. Riley practiced drawing them all the time. He was very good at making rainbows. If only Riley was good at not being afraid.

Riley's mom, dad, and big sister, Samantha, walked with him down the hall toward Great-grandma's room.

Great-grandma was not herself lately. She was weak and could not walk. Her thoughts did not always make sense. She forgot things a lot. Mom said Great-grandma might even forget his name. But Riley wanted to see her anyway—at first.

Riley walked slower—and *slower*—and **s l o w e r.**

Great-grandma called Riley her "sweet boy." She said he was the best artist in the whole world. Riley wanted to give her this picture. It was his best work so far. But what if Great-grandma forgot she liked his pictures? What if she frowned and crumpled it up with her shaky hands?

Riley stopped walking.

Samantha noticed first.

"Mom, Dad," she said, "Riley's not coming."

"Riley," said Mom, "what's wrong?"

Riley looked at his feet.

Mom knelt beside him.

"I'm afraid," he whispered.

"Ohhh," said Mom, "I understand. It's hard when someone you love changes. Great-grandma's weaker and a little confused, but she won't look too different. I know it seems scary, but we'll be right beside you."

"And," said Dad, pointing to Riley's picture, "so will God. Remember His promise from Philippians, 'I can do *everything* through him who gives me strength.'"

Mom stood up and Riley took her hand.

Riley thought a prayer to God as they walked into Great-grandma's room. *Please help me be strong today. And help me not be afraid.*

Great-grandma loved his picture. She smiled so big—just like she used to. She didn't remember his name, but she did say, "Oh, there's my *sweet boy.*"

Riley knew he'd helped Great-grandma have a wonderful day. And that made Riley feel very strong! God really does keep His promises!

Now go back to the big picture and tell what Riley learned about Philippians 4:13.

MEMORY BOOSTERS

★ Talk with your child about his biggest challenges. Write the words "I can _____ with Jesus" on sticky notes. Place a note near each challenging area (on the computer because it's hard to turn it off when Dad says to). Have your child say Philippians 4:13 each time he sees a note.

★ Make barbells with empty paper towel rolls, newspaper, and large aluminum foil. Roll newspaper into "balls." Position a ball at each end of tube. Wrap with foil until sturdy. Say Philippians 4:13 while "exercising."

I CAN DO EVERYTHING

Chorus:
I can do everything
Through Him who gives me strength
I can do everything
Through Him who gives me strength

I will be more caring
I can pray for those in need
I will thank God for His promises
I just have to believe
Philippians 4:13

(Repeat chorus)

God's power makes me strong
To forgive someone who hurt me
I do not have to be afraid
Because God will never leave me
Philippians 4:13

(Repeat chorus twice)

Words and Music by Scott and Cathy Liebenow

Honor Your Parents

Honor your father and your mother. EXODUS 20:12

IN A MINUTE

Marcus loved camping near Silver Lake with his mom and dad. They hiked through the woods, roasted marshmallows, and slept in their tent. Best of all, Marcus swam and played on the beach.

"Look at my sandcastle," Marcus told his mom. "It has a stone bridge."

"It's great," Mom agreed as she put some sandwiches, apples, and juice boxes away.

"Pick up the paper plates and napkins, please," Mom said to Marcus.

"In a minute," Marcus answered. "I have to find some leaves for my castle roof first." Then Marcus climbed a sandy hill nearby. He picked some leaves from the bottom branch of a tree and found an inchworm.

"Marcus," called Dad, "don't forget to put away your sand toys and beach ball."

"In a minute," answered Marcus. "This inchworm is climbing on my finger right now." It tickled his skin as it crept along.

Suddenly, the wind started to blow. It tugged at Marcus's shirt and blew the napkins, plates, and sand toys, too.

"Help!" called Mom as the napkins flew off like little kites. She tried to grab a handful.

"Hurry up!" called Dad as the beach ball bounced into the waves and sand toys tumbled across the beach.

Marcus raced to help. He caught a plate, but another swooshed past him. Some sailed under the picnic table.

Marcus, Mom, and Dad ran in every direction. They caught the plates, napkins, and toys and tossed them into the tent. Finally, they stopped to rest and Marcus looked at the mess. It was everything that he had been asked to pick up, but he hadn't listened.

"I'm sorry," Marcus told his mom and dad. "Next time, I'll do a better job of obeying."

"OK," agreed Dad. "Now let's clean up this mess together."

A moment later a boy stopped by their tent. "Is this your beach ball?" he asked. "I found it in the waves."

"Yes," said Marcus. "Thanks."

"I'm Gabe," said the boy. "Do you want to play catch?"

Marcus almost said, "Yes," but then he smiled. "In a minute," he told Gabe. "I have to help my mom and dad first."

Now go back to the big picture and tell what Marcus learned about Exodus 20:12.

MEMORY BOOSTERS

★ Help your child cut out a paper tree trunk with bare branches. Then make leaves of many different colors. Write a Bible verse on each leaf. Allow your child to choose a verse each week to memorize.

★ Have family members write the words to Exodus 20:12 at the top of a piece of paper. Say the words together. Then talk about how God wants us to honor each other, too! Make a list of people that God wants us to honor and talk about ways to honor them.

HONOR YOUR FATHER AND MOTHER

Moses went up a mountain (Mt. Sinai)
And God gave him ten laws
To help the Israelites overcome their flaws
Today we're gonna learn one of the ten
Now we're gonna sing it again and again

Chorus:
Honor your father and mother
Honor your father and mother
Exodus 20:12 says to
Honor your father and mother

Moms and dads aren't perfect
But they really try their best
If you obey your parents
God says you will be blessed
I know they make you eat your veggies
    before your desserts
But you really need to remember this verse

(Repeat chorus twice)

Words and Music by Scott and Cathy Liebenow

God's Word in My Heart

I have hidden your word in my heart that I might not sin against you.
PSALM 119:11

WHAT'S THE RECIPE?

Mackenzie and Madison couldn't wait to bake cookies with Auntie! Then the doorbell rang.

"Oh, no," groaned Madison.

"Oh, no," moaned Mackenzie.

"Don't worry," said Auntie, "I'll be right back."

Several minutes later, Madison said, "Since we're Auntie's helpers, let's put the flour in the bowl." She tipped the flour bag and gave it a pat. **Poof!** Flour puffed into the bowl *and* up on the girls' faces.

"Cookies need salt and sugar, too," said Madison. She scooped in equal amounts of salt and sugar.

"Ooooo," said Mackenzie, "it looks like snow!"

Next, Madison dumped in baking soda and dropped in some butter. Then she announced, "Finally, chocolate chips!" as she plopped several in her mouth, gave a few to Mackenzie, and tossed some in the bowl.

They took turns stirring. "Something's wrong," said Mackenzie.

Madison tasted the mix on her spoon. **"YUCK!"** She threw the spoon and stomped her feet.

"Madison!" said Auntie. Two flour-white faces turned red.

"The Bible says, 'When you are angry, do not sin.' Throwing things when you're angry is not right."

"I'm sorry, Auntie," said Madison.

"I forgive you," said Auntie.

"You do? But I made a mess," said Madison.

"God's Word says, 'Forgive as the Lord forgave you.' *Why* are you angry anyway?"

"Our cookie dough tastes terrible!"

"Did you follow the recipe?" asked Auntie.

"You don't use a recipe," said Madison.

"I am following a recipe," said Auntie. "It's memorized. I've read it many times before and used it so often that I just know it."

"It's in your heart," said Mackenzie.

"That reminds me of another verse," said Auntie. "'I have hidden your Word in my heart that I might not sin against you.'"

"How do you remember so many Bible verses?" asked Mackenzie.

"It's like my recipe, sweetie," said Auntie. "I read the verses many times and use them so often that they're in my head *and* in my heart when I need them! Now, are you ready to start over?"

"Really?" squeaked Madison.

"Yes, and this time we'll add vanilla and eggs, too," said Auntie.

"Ohhhh," nodded the girls.

"And," said Auntie, "we'll use the right amount of each ingredient— in the right order. Knowing the recipe and following it exactly makes *all* the difference in the world!"

Now go back to the big picture and tell what Madison and Mackenzie learned about Psalm 119:11.

MEMORY BOOSTERS

★ Make "warning signs." Use crayons and blank paper. How does God's Word protect us, warn us, and direct us? Say Psalm 119:11 together. Hang the signs as reminders and say the verse each time you pass by them.

★ Repeat Psalm 119:11 several times together. Now you say it, leaving out a word. Did your child catch you? Repeat it again. Explain how we need **ALL** the words to know God's thoughts.

I HAVE HIDDEN YOUR WORD

I will obey
Obey Your Word
Your Word is what is living in me
And I will learn
I'll learn Your Word
Your Word is what is living in me

Chorus:
I have hidden Your Word in my heart
That I might not sin against You
I have hidden Your Word in my heart
That I might not sin against You
Psalm 119:11

I know this much
This much is true
I want to live my life for You
When I'm at home
Or I'm at school
I want to live my life for You

(Repeat chorus twice)

Words and Music by Scott and Cathy Liebenow

Love Your Neighbor

Love your neighbor as yourself. MATTHEW 22:39

LOST IN LEFT FIELD

Rashid threw the ball to second base. "Good throw," said his teammate Mitchell.

"Thanks," said Rashid. He liked being on the T-ball team.

"Oh, no. Katie's batting," Mitchell groaned. "She'll be lucky if she hits the ball."

"Turn sideways," Coach said as Katie hit the T-ball stand. "Try again."

Katie scrunched up her face and swung the bat. This time she hit the ball, but she twisted around and landed in a heap. Everyone laughed.

"Good hit," said Coach, but Katie didn't look happy.

Rashid watched the next three batters, but not many balls came to left field. After a while, Rashid pretended he was an acrobat and tumbled around.

"Time for our snack," Coach called.

Rashid stood up and stuck his hand in his pocket to find his favorite rock. He wanted to show Mitchell.

"My rock!" cried Rashid as he felt his empty pocket. "I lost it!"

Mitchell helped Rashid look for a minute. Then he said, "You can always find another rock," and ran off.

Rashid kept looking; he didn't want a snack.

"Come on," some of his teammates called. "Don't worry about a silly rock."

Rashid didn't listen.

Soon Katie walked over. "I'll help you," she said. "What does your rock look like?"

"It's shiny and red," explained Rashid.

Katie searched with Rashid, but they still didn't find his rock. Finally, it was time to go. Rashid felt like he had a lump stuck in his throat.

"Wait," Katie said. "I have a rock for you. It's a fossil. See the place where a leaf used to be? I have a whole collection at home."

"It's so cool," said Rashid. "I love rocks."

"Me, too," said Katie. "I like spaceships, too. I want to be an astronaut—not a baseball player!"

Rashid laughed. "I love stars," he said, "and I have a new telescope."

"Wow," said Katie, happy to hear this great news.

"Would you like to come and see it?" asked Rashid. Katie's clumsiness suddenly didn't matter anymore.

"Sure," Katie agreed.

Rashid didn't even notice when Katie tripped over her laces. He lost his rock in left field, but he found a new friend.

Now go back to the big picture and tell what Rashid learned about Matthew 22:39.

MEMORY BOOSTERS

★ Gather several smooth stones. Write each word of Matthew 22:39 on its own stone. Have your child place the stones in order and read the verse aloud. For variation, add words such as "dog," "fish," "music," etc., to switch in and out as you discuss what it means to love your neighbor.

★ Write the words of Matthew 22:39 across the top of poster board. Say it together. Allow each member of the family to put on the poster at least one way she can love a neighbor. Hang up the poster. Use it as a reminder to **REALLY** love your neighbors.

LOVE YOUR NEIGHBOR

Chorus:
Love your neighbor as yourself
Love your neighbor as yourself
Love your neighbor as yourself
'Cuz God loves everyone

(Repeat chorus)

Well if God can find the good in me
Then maybe He can help me see
That everyone is special in their own way
And judging isn't up to me

So how do you wanna be treated? (echo)
Remember Matthew 22:39

(Repeat chorus)

So even if the day doesn't go my way
I know that I should still be nice
God wants me to love everyone
And be the best example of Christ

So how do you wanna be treated? (echo)
Remember Matthew 22:39

(Repeat chorus twice)

God loves everyone

Words and Music by Scott Liebenow

Preach the Good News

He said to them, "Go into all the world and preach the good news to all creation." MARK 16:15

AN AMERICAN MISSIONARY

Lela beamed with excitement when she heard the news! Missionaries were coming to her small town for the summer and they had a daughter her age! Wow! She couldn't imagine how wonderful this girl must be. She probably has the whole Bible memorized, speaks five languages, can name every continent, and wears tribal clothes just like the natives.

Every evening found Lela imagining life as a missionary's daughter. Going from village to village telling about Jesus must be very exciting! She could hardly wait to meet the new girl!

Finally, the big day arrived. Lela went to the airport with her parents to greet the missionary family. Off the plane came several American-looking families. *They must be in the back,* Lela said to herself.

But one of the families walked right up to them. They introduced themselves and Lela was surprised at how Stephanie was dressed. Both girls were wearing blue jeans and had ponytails!

Lela and Stephanie immediately became friends. They enjoyed laughing together and telling each other everything about themselves. In the weeks that followed, Lela learned that she and Stephanie were alike in many ways.

They both played with dolls and liked to jump rope. Stephanie spoke only English but could repeat a few phrases from Zimbabwe. She went to a school like Lela's and always dressed in American clothes!

As the summer came to an end, Lela and Stephanie grew sad. They promised to e-mail every week.

As Lela said "Good-bye" she began to cry. Stephanie hugged her and said, "Remember, we're here to share the good news with everyone! You share it in America and I will share it in Africa!"

Suddenly, Lela understood. She was a missionary too—an American missionary!

The e-mails began. In one e-mail Lela wrote, "I told a new girl at school about a pizza party at my church. She is going to come! Her name is Whitney."

Stephanie replied, "My cousin, Kollette, and I took care of a sick baby today while our parents talked with the baby's mom. They told her about Jesus and gave her some medicine to help the baby. Please pray for the baby and her mom."

Lela was glad to know that she didn't have to live in another country to be a missionary. She could be a missionary by sharing God with the people in her town!

Now go back to the big picture and tell what Lela learned about Mark 16:15.

MEMORY BOOSTERS

★ Write the words for Mark 16:15 on an inflated balloon. Each time you tap the balloon to keep it in the air, say another word of the Bible verse. If the balloon falls, start over again. Try to keep the balloon in the air long enough to finish the entire verse.

★ As you drive or walk around the neighborhood with your family, talk about the many places where you can tell others the good news. For example, say the words of Mark 16:15 and follow up with, "and to my friends at school."

GO INTO ALL THE WORLD

Spreading the good news is the thing to do
Listen to what Jesus said to His whole crew
He said to them

Chorus:
Go into all the world
And preach the good news to all creation
Go into all the world
And preach the good news to all creation
Mark 16:15

Try to reach out into your neighborhood
Sharing God's love 'cuz Jesus said we should
Tell everyone

(Repeat chorus)

Mark 16:15 (echo)
Mark 16:15 (echo)
Now whisper
Mark 16:15 (echo)
Mark 16:15 (echo)

(Repeat chorus)

Mark 16:15

Words and Music by Scott Liebenow

Be Kind to Others

Do to others as you would have them do to you. LUKE 6:31

MUSEUM MANIA

"Mom, are we almost there?" asked Thomas for the third time. Thomas and his little brother, Michael, sat in the back seat of their van, stretching their necks as they looked for the Children's Museum.

"Almost," their mom called back. After one more red light, Thomas and Michael finally saw the half-dome shape of the museum.

"Yeah!" they called. "We're here! We're here!"

As they walked in, Mom reminded them of the rules. "Boys, be kind to each other and to other kids—treat them like you want to be treated—or we'll leave early!" Thomas and Michael nodded. They loved going to the museum and did not want to leave early.

The boys spotted the ball playroom and ran ahead. There were walls of nets and purple, blue, yellow, and green balls flying everywhere. Thomas and Michael threw balls into a basketball hoop. Then the balls traveled along the ceiling in a clear tube and dropped into a giant bin.

Next stop—waterworks! The boys got wet even with plastic smocks on as they built water pipes, floated boats, and squirted a windmill to make it turn.

As Mom took the boys to the water fountain, they chattered about what to do next. "First we'll go to the construction site, then the building blocks, and then the giant fire truck!" Thomas said.

"Yeah, the fire truck," Michael echoed.

"Remember to be kind," Mom called after them as they ran toward the bright yellow construction crane. The boys wanted to operate the

crane and make it move large blocks around. Both boys reached the controls at the same time.

"I got here first," Thomas said.

"No, me!" said Michael, squeezing in front of his brother.

"No, me first!" Thomas shouted, pushing Michael back. Michael began crying.

Mom ran up and took both boys by the hands. "Now we're leaving early," she said sternly as they walked toward the door. "Do you know why?"

"We weren't being kind," Thomas said.

"Right," said Mom, "and now you've lost your chance for more playtime at the museum. Always be kind and treat people the way you want them to treat you. That's what the Bible says, and that's what God wants us to do."

As they rode home, Thomas and Michael knew that next time they would work harder to be kind.

Now go back to the big picture and tell what Thomas and Michael learned about Luke 6:31.

MEMORY BOOSTERS

★ Make a mini-poster of the words from Luke 6:31. Write the words on a piece of white paper. Then provide various materials with which to decorate the poster. As you work together, encourage your child to talk about how she can treat others the way she wants to be treated.

★ Make up "calling cards." Write on them, "'Do to others as you would have them do to you.' I am giving you this card because I want to do something kind for you. Now, please do a kind deed for someone else and pass the card along." Do something kind for everyone you hand a card to!

BE KIND TO OTHERS

Do all of your chores (I did it)
Bake your neighbor cookies (Yummy)
Tell someone you love them (I love you)
Share your toys with a smile (Here you go)

Chorus:
Do to others as you would have them do
    to you
This is Luke 6:31

Take out the trash (Yuk)
Be nice to your teacher (Please may I)
Set the dinner table (Dinner is served)
Give your mom a kiss (Smooch)

(Repeat chorus twice)

Words and Music by Scott and Cathy Liebenow

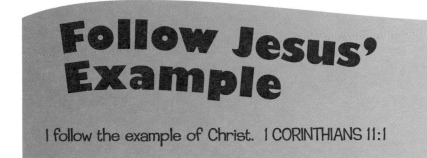

Follow Jesus' Example

I follow the example of Christ. 1 CORINTHIANS 11:1

TROUBLE IN THE TUBES

Shanice gulped down her milk and gobbled up her cheeseburger. She couldn't wait to finish eating so she could crawl through the colored tubes!

"Bye Mom," Shanice called as she quickly took off her shoes and began climbing up into the bright blue, green, red, and yellow tubes. Up, up, and up she climbed—until she got to the top. Whoosh! Shanice flew down the slide and landed on her feet, laughing.

She ran to the opening and began climbing again. This time she went higher, peeking out a window to wave at her mom below. She slid down another slide and landed in a hidden area in the middle of the tubes play area.

"Move! We don't need any baby girls in here!"

Shanice turned to see who had said those mean words. She saw a little girl trying not to cry as two older boys teased her. One boy pushed the girl backwards, "Hey baby, are you gonna cry for your momma?"

Shanice held very still. She didn't want the mean boys to look her way. She knew she should help, but she was afraid of the boys teasing and pushing her, too.

Another boy saw what the boys were doing; maybe he would help. But the boy quickly climbed back into the tubes.

At that moment, Shanice remembered what she had learned about Jesus. Jesus loved everyone, even people others didn't want to be around. Jesus *always* helped the people no one else wanted to help.

Shanice knew that she should follow Jesus' example and help the little girl.

"That's enough!" Shanice said in her biggest voice as she walked toward the boys. "Leave her alone; she's smaller than you."

"Oh yeah? Well, you're a baby, too," said one of the boys. But the boys crawled back up into the tubes and left the girls alone.

"Hi, my name's Shanice, what's yours?"

"Hailey," said the girl, sniffling.

"Don't worry about those boys. Let's go down the slide together," Shanice said.

"OK," said Hailey, smiling.

They climbed up, up, and up to the top of the slide and giggled all the way down as blue, green, red, and yellow tubes blurred into one big, happy rainbow.

Now go back to the big picture and tell what Shanice learned about 1 Corinthians 11:1.

MEMORY BOOSTERS

★ Play a game of charades. Choose actions that show how you can follow Christ. Start by saying, "I follow the example of Christ by _____." Then pretend to rake leaves, love your friends, obey Dad, wash dishes, etc.

★ Once your child has a good number of Bible verses memorized, make a memory game. Write each verse on its own card. Write each reference on a separate card. Turn the cards over, mix them up, and try to match each verse with its reference.

MY EXAMPLE

Chorus:
I follow the example of Christ
I follow the example of Christ
First Corinthians eleven, verse one
I follow the example of Christ

(Repeat chorus)

What would Jesus do
That's what I should do
Say what He would say
Each and every day
Jesus lived a perfect life
And showed us what to do
Places He would go
Friends that He would know
That's what I will do as I follow Jesus Christ

(Repeat chorus twice)

When I need a friend to the very end
He is always there and He really cares
Nothing could be finer than to follow Jesus
   Christ
I will live for Him through the thick and thin
That's what I will do as I follow Jesus Christ

(Repeat chorus quietly, loudly, slowly, quickly)

Words and Music by Scott Graffius

Fruit of the Spirit

The fruit of the Spirit is love, joy, peace, patience, kindness, goodness, faithfulness, gentleness and self-control. GALATIANS 5:22, 23

HEDGEHOGS AND SUNSHINE

Tyler's day didn't start with a smile. First, his sister ate the last waffle so he had to eat cornflakes. Then he spilled orange juice on his pants and his cereal got soggy. Tyler finally went to school, but he felt as grumpy and prickly as a hedgehog.

After hanging up his jacket, Tyler wanted to make clay dinosaurs with his friend David. But David was drawing airplanes.

"Tyler, come and help me," called his friend Kayla. "I can't find the right pieces for this puzzle."

"Don't ask me," grumbled Tyler. He didn't feel like helping anyone.

Kayla didn't smile. She tried again and then pushed the pieces into a little pile.

A moment later the block tower Carlos was building began to wobble.

"Kayla," called Carlos. "Come and help me."

"Don't ask me," grumbled Kayla. She didn't feel like helping anyone either.

Crash! Carlos's block tower tumbled down and knocked over Ben's block castle.

"Look what happened!" cried Ben. "Now I have to build my castle again."

"Don't ask me to help," grumbled Carlos.

Finally, it was snack time. The teacher passed out milk and crackers. When Jeff reached for a cracker he knocked over his milk carton.

The milk spilled into a puddle and ran over the edges of his desk.

"Will someone please get some napkins?" Jeff asked.

"Don't ask me," grumbled Ben, Carlos, and Kayla.

"Don't ask me," said some other students.

Suddenly, Tyler realized that his "don't ask me" attitude had spilled everywhere, just like Jeff's milk. The whole room was full of prickly hedgehogs.

Tyler jumped up and grabbed a napkin. "I'll help," he said, trying to be kind.

"Thanks," Jeff said as Tyler wiped up the milk.

"No problem," said Tyler, and he felt a little better. Then he spotted Kayla's puzzle. If he were to be patient, he could help her, too.

"Come on, Kayla," Tyler said. "Let's put your puzzle together."

"I'll help, too," smiled Jeff.

"Me, too!" Carlos said.

Everyone hurried over to help and Tyler laughed. His "I'll help" attitude made him feel as happy and warm as a bright ray of sunshine.

Now go back to the big picture and tell what Tyler learned about Galatians 5:22, 23.

MEMORY BOOSTERS

★ Cut out various fruit shapes. On each piece of fruit, write one word from Galatians 5:22, 23. Hide the fruit around the house. Once all have been found, put the words in order and say the verse. Post the fruit in key places or put them in a basket on the kitchen table.

★ Enjoy making a wonderful fruit salad with your family. As you peel, cut, chop, and scoop, talk about the fruit of the Spirit God has planted in our hearts. Say the Bible verse and pray that people will see godly fruit in your lives.

THE FRUIT OF THE SPIRIT

Love, joy, peace, patience, kindness, goodness,
    faithfulness, gentleness and self-control (Repeat)

It is so hard to have fun when someone's rude
Nobody likes sour grapes or a bad attitude
God gave us special fruit for us to grow
They're not treats for us to eat
They're for us to show
This kind of fruit
It does not fall from a tree
It is from Galatians 5:22 and 23

Chorus:
The fruit of the spirit is love, joy, peace, patience.
    kindness, goodness, faithfulness, gentleness and
    self-control (Repeat)

Look in your heart and ask yourself "how am I
    behaving"
Are all my friends having fun or are they leaving
The Bible names God's special fruit just to remind us
This is the way to behave with loving-kindness
This kind of fruit
It does not fall from a tree
It is from Galatians 5:22 and 23

(Repeat chorus 4 times)

Words and Music by Scott and Cathy Liebenow

Forgive Each Other

Be kind and compassionate to one another, forgiving each other, just as in Christ God forgave you. EPHESIANS 4:32

EASIER THAN YOU THINK

Evan and his next-door neighbor Jacob spent their summer days swimming, swinging, and catching fireflies. Every day they made new plans for fun. One day things were different. Evan invited another friend over to swim and didn't call Jacob. *He doesn't like swimming that much anyway. He won't care,* thought Evan. So all day Evan splashed in the pool with Preston.

Next door, Jacob sat on his swing listening to the laughter. He felt sad and wanted to play. Jacob's feelings were hurt, so he called another friend to stay all night. That evening Jacob and Mikie ran through the yard laughing and catching fireflies.

Evan's friend Preston had gone home and now Evan sat on his porch feeling sad. He loved catching fireflies with Jacob. How could Jacob have invited someone else to stay all night instead of him?

The next day Evan swam by himself. Jacob played on his swings by himself. "Why aren't you playing with Jacob?" Evan's mom asked.

"Jacob invited Mikie to stay all night and didn't ask me. I don't want to be his friend anymore."

Evan's mom knew that he didn't really mean this. She looked at him and said, "Now, Evan, didn't you have Preston over to swim the other day? You didn't even think about asking Jacob to join you."

"But Jacob doesn't like to swim that much, Mom. He didn't care," Evan quickly replied.

"Are you sure?" Evan's mom asked.

Evan thought for a moment. He knew that he didn't mean to hurt Jacob. He had ignored Jacob when Preston was over and then expected Jacob to remember him when Mikie was at his house. He asked his mom, "What should I do? I want to be Jacob's friend."

"You should go see him," she said.

Evan was nervous as he walked to Jacob's door. *Saying "I'm sorry" is hard. What if Jacob doesn't forgive me?*

Evan knocked hesitantly on the door. When Jacob opened the door, he seemed glad to see Evan. Jacob talked before Evan could have a chance.

"I'm sorry for inviting Mikie over to stay all night and not asking you to come, too. I know you like catching fireflies. I was just mad that you didn't ask me over when Preston was at your house."

Evan began to laugh. Jacob was confused. Why would Evan laugh when Jacob was trying to say he was sorry?

When Evan explained why he was at Jacob's house, Jacob realized that they were trying to say "I'm sorry" to each other at the same time! They both learned that forgiving each other was the right thing to do and saying "I'm sorry" wasn't as hard as either one of them had thought.

Now go back to the big picture and tell what Evan and Jacob learned about Ephesians 4:32.

MEMORY BOOSTERS

★ On a piece of large card stock, write the words for Ephesians 4:32. Decorate the design as desired. Cut the paper into several pieces, making a puzzle. Each time the puzzle is completed, say the Bible verse.

★ Every time you see a firefly, say Ephesians 4:32 together. Recall the story of Evan and Jacob. Encourage family members to share their own stories of compassion and forgiveness.

BE KIND AND COMPASSIONATE

What do you do
When others are mean to you
Try to do what Jesus did
That's to forgive and forget
So what is the answer
Do you know
Read Ephesians 4:32

Chorus:
Be kind and compassionate to one another
Forgiving each other
Just as in Christ
God forgave you

If someone's mean
But they say they're sorry to you
Don't turn your back
Don't still be mad
That's not what God wants you to do
So what is the answer
Do you know
Read Ephesians 4:32
We've said it already for you

(Repeat chorus twice)

Words and Music by Scott Liebenow

INDEX OF STORIES

INDEX OF SONGS

Welcome to the Family!

Heritage Builders®
Helping You Build a Family of Faith

We hope you've enjoyed this book. Heritage Builders was founded in 1995 by three fathers with a passion for the next generation. As a new ministry of Focus on the Family, Heritage Builders strives to equip, train, and motivate parents to become intentional about building a strong spiritual heritage.

It's quite a challenge for busy parents to find ways to build a spiritual foundation for their families—especially in a way they enjoy and understand. Through activities and participation, children can learn biblical truth in a way they can understand, enjoy— and *remember.*

Passing along a heritage of Christian faith to your family is a parent's highest calling. Heritage Builders' goal is to encourage and empower you in this great mission with practical resources and inspiring ideas that really work—and help your children develop a lasting love for God.

* * *

How To Reach Us

For more information, visit our Heritage Builders Web site! Log on to **www.heritagebuilders.com** to discover new resources, sample activities, and ideas to help you pass on a spiritual heritage. To request any of these resources, simply call Focus on the Family at 1-800-A-FAMILY (1-800-232-6459) or in Canada, call 1-800-661-9800. Or send your request to Focus on the Family, Colorado Springs, CO 80995. In Canada, write Focus on the Family, P.O. Box 9800, Stn. Terminal, Vancouver, B.C. V6B 4G3

To learn more about Focus on the Family or to find out if there is an associate office in your country, please visit www.family.org

We'd love to hear from you!